The Journey Home

Living Humbly
Amid Suffering

KRESS
BIBLICAL
RESOURCES

Richard Caldwell

D1636785

The Journey Home: Living Humbly Amid Suffering

Copyright © 2022 Richard Caldwell

Published by:
Kress Biblical Resources
www.kressbiblical.com

ISBN: 978-1-934952-71-9

Printed in Colombia

Contents

THE LIFE OF
TRUE HUMILITY

A Study of James 4

James 4

1 What causes quarrels and what causes fights among you? Is it not this, that your passions are at war within you? **2** You desire and do not have, so you murder. You covet and cannot obtain, so you fight and quarrel. You do not have, because you do not ask. **3** You ask and do not receive, because you ask wrongly, to spend it on your passions. **4** You adulterous people! Do you not know that friendship with the world is enmity with God? Therefore whoever wishes to be a friend of the world makes himself an enemy of God. **5** Or do you suppose it is to no purpose that the Scripture says, "He yearns jealously over the spirit that he has made to dwell in us"? **6** But he gives more grace. Therefore it says, "God opposes the proud but gives grace to the humble." **7** Submit yourselves therefore to God. Resist the devil, and he will flee from you. **8** Draw near to God, and he will draw near to you. Cleanse your hands, you sinners, and purify your hearts, you double-minded. **9** Be wretched and mourn and weep. Let your laughter be turned to mourning and your joy to gloom. **10** Humble yourselves before the Lord, and he will exalt you.

11 Do not speak evil against one another, brothers. The one who speaks against a brother or judges his brother, speaks evil against the law and judges the law. But if you judge the law, you are not a doer of the law but a judge. **12** There is only one lawgiver and judge, he who is able to save and to destroy. But who are you to judge your neighbor?

13 Come now, you who say, "Today or tomorrow we will go into such and such a town and spend a year there and trade and make a profit"—[14] yet you do not know what tomorrow will bring. What is your life? For you are a mist that appears for a little time and then vanishes. [15] Instead you ought to say, "If the Lord wills, we will live and do this or that." [16] As it is, you boast in your arrogance. All such boasting is evil. [17] So whoever knows the right thing to do and fails to do it, for him it is sin

.

What Is Humility?

The theme of humility is at the very heart of the fourth chapter in the book of James and is woven throughout it in various ways. There are few subjects more important than this one. Notice the centerpiece of the chapter, verse 6: *But he gives more grace. Therefore it says, "God opposes the proud but gives grace to the humble."* Humility is also seen repeatedly in verses 10-17.

When you consider what verse 6 says, that *God opposes the proud, but He gives grace to the humble*, you want to walk in humility, don't you! What is pride, and what is humility? You don't want to be standing in the place where God is opposed to you, but desire to be living a life that He is able to bless, and able to pour out His grace upon. That makes this subject vital, and you'll want to know what humility is and how to walk in it. Once you understand the importance of humility, you're not surprised when Satan attacks you at this very point. You can bank on the fact that Satan is going to attempt to distort whatever is important.

In Proverbs 6:16-17, God says there are six things that He hates, seven things that are an abomination to Him. First on the list is haughty eyes, pride. You want to know what God hates and to avoid it. You want to know what God loves, what He's pleased with, and to walk in it.

I have had the privilege of shepherding people for many years, and this is an area where I've seen a lot of confusion among God's people. Sometimes they are confused about what pride is, what humility really is, and what it really looks like.

<u>The core of humility is submission to God.</u> This means an obedient life, one rightly informed (seeing both God and ourselves rightly), measured by the standard of Scripture. We must truly understand and embrace that. True humility will never be pursued when we are congratulating ourselves or flagellating ourselves based on false perspectives of what humility really is.

Reflection and Application

1. Have you ever met a truly humble person? Without gossiping, what made you think the person was humble?
2. Have you ever met a person with false humility? (Don't name names.) Without gossiping, what made you think the person was not truly humble?
3. Before reading in this book, have you thought about a connection between humility and obedience?

Some Common Misconceptions About Humility

Humility Is Not a Certain Personality

One way that people commonly misunderstand humility is to equate humility with a certain kind of personality. It can be expressed, and is expressed THROUGH personalities, but it isn't to be equated with a certain kind of personality. Perhaps someone has a small personality, or a reserved personality, or someone is quiet, then we immediately conclude that he's humble. And if someone has a large, unmistakable personality, then we might conclude he is proud, because he's not as quiet, and he may speak more than others. If you're not careful, in the life of a church, everyone begins to look the same, talk the same, walk the same, because they have bought into this mistake.

One evidence that you can't come to that conclusion, is shown in the perfect wisdom of our Savior when He chose His disciples. Some very quiet and unassuming people are very proud by the standard of what God can see. And some people are like Peter. At times, they say exactly the wrong thing, or do the most dreadful thing, but they are the first ones into the water when they see the Lord standing on the beach. Our Lord chose eleven disciples, eleven true disciples. Those eleven men were quite a group of personalities. Out of those eleven with their vibrant personalities, the Lord chose three of them to form His inner circle, Peter, James and John. Remember the nickname for James and John—Sons of thunder.

The one that He gave a special prominence to, Peter, is the one that we associate with foot-in-mouth disease. He's the one who always had something to say, the one who always spoke up for the group and the one who failed in ways that make us all feel embarrassed at times. We're wrong to conclude that just because someone has a quieter personality it necessarily means that they're humble. Conversely, just because someone has a livelier personality, it does not necessarily mean that they're proud.

Read John 21:1-8 to be reminded of Peter's eagerness to see Jesus. Even though Peter had some unmistakable failures, he was the first one in the water when he saw Jesus standing on the beach.

John 21:1 *After this Jesus revealed himself again to the disciples by the Sea of Tiberias, and he revealed himself in this way. ² Simon Peter, Thomas (called the Twin), Nathanael of Cana in Galilee, the sons of Zebedee, and two others of his disciples were together. ³ Simon Peter said to them, "I am going fishing." They said to him, "We will go with you." They went out and got into the boat, but that night they caught nothing. ⁴ Just as day was breaking, Jesus stood on the shore; yet the disciples did not know that it was Jesus. ⁵ Jesus said to them, "Children, do you have any fish?" They answered him, "No." ⁶He said to them, "Cast the net on the right side of the boat, and you will find some." So they cast it, and now they were not able to haul it in, because of the quantity of fish. ⁷ That disciple whom Jesus loved therefore said to Peter, "It is the Lord!" When Simon Peter heard that it was the Lord, he put on his outer garment, for he was stripped for work, and threw himself into the sea. ⁸ The* *other disciples came in the boat, dragging the net full of fish, for they were not far from the land, but about a hundred yards off.*

Besides Peter, John mentions Thomas and Nathanael. After the Resurrection, Thomas is resistant. "I'm not going to believe unless I see the wounds in His hands and in His side." Nathanael is the one who had said years earlier, "What good can come out of Nazareth?" These men are not wallflowers!

The rest of the men act in a sane fashion. "We're going to stay in the boat. We're going to bring the fish." Although Peter was characterized by some major failures, he was also characterized by what Jesus produced in him, even while his unique personality was preserved and useful in the hand of God. And so, the man that we often associate with great failure, we ought to also associate with great love. Jesus saw something in Peter that perhaps some of us would not have seen.

Humility Is Not Chiefly About External Demeanor

Sometimes we equate humility with personality, but sometimes we equate humility with external demeanor. This is similar to what I've just described, but a little bit different. That is, if you're not careful you associate humility with the way someone carries themselves, with facial expressions, or with tone of voice. When we begin to equate humility with this, people try to embody what they perceive to be the demeanor that belongs to humility.

I'll never forget a time years ago when I was a youth pastor at a particular church. I'd been there for about a year when a man walked up to me and said, "I need to ask you for forgiveness." And I said, "Why?" And he said, "Well, because I misjudged you." He said, "I thought you were a proud person."

Well, we're all struggling with pride. Are we not? So, he wouldn't have been wrong to conclude that I struggled with pride. He wasn't wrong about that, but he went on to say, "I thought you were a proud person because of the way you walked." What does that do to you? Immediately you're thinking, "All right. How was I walking? How do I change that?"

My point is this: if you associate humility with some sort of external behavior, you may have the wrong criterion, and may draw wrong conclusions. I'm not denying that pride can be manifested in some of those things. The Bible talks about a haughty look, etc., but you can't EQUATE humility with those behaviors. That's precisely what hypocrites do. Those behaviors aren't really the essence of humility, and they can be easily feigned.

Notice what Jesus said about the Pharisees who wanted everyone to see that they were fasting—which was associated with humility:

Matthew 6:16 *"And when you fast, do not look gloomy like the hypocrites, for they disfigure their faces that their fasting may be seen by others. Truly, I say to you, they have received their reward."*

I've sometimes said to people, **stop trying to act humble, and ask God to make you humble.** Stop trying to act humble and choose humility — be humble.

Humility Is Not Self-Preoccupation

There's a third common misconception concerning humility: Humility is all about self-awareness, conscious about itself. The truly humble person constantly searches within himself, within herself, looking for every ounce of pride that exists in order to kill it.

When this is your perception of humility, you may become characterized by self-deprecation. "Let me run myself down. Let me tell you everything that's wrong with me, every way that I fail, every way that I fall short. Let me demonstrate that my heart is humble, while letting everybody else know that I don't view myself highly."

Someone has said that pride is a sin best slain indirectly. I think what they meant is this: Knowing that pride is a great sin, that God hates it, and saying, "I want to deal with whatever pride is in my life," is appropriate, and that's dealing with it directly. It's knowing that God loves humility, meets with us in the place of humility, and saying, "I will humble myself. God, as You set it forth for me in Your Word, I will humble myself." But understand that humbling yourself is not achieved by pride hunting, but by submitting to truth and by putting to death anything that doesn't accord with the truth. **Humility looks to God and looks away from itself.** You're not going to discover the pride in your life by going on a pride search. You need to remember this:

every sin you've ever committed has had pride in it. There isn't a sin that you and I commit that isn't proud. So, **if you want to kill pride, kill sin.**

The more you make pride your focus, instead of submission to God, the more prone you'll be to blind spots in your life about pride. In fact, you may find yourself very proud of your humility. That's why pride is a sin best slain indirectly.

That's not denying that pride itself is sin, but there's nothing more characteristic of pride than its refusal to deal with sin. It is defiant against God, and there's nothing more characteristic of pride than that it is anthropocentric, that is, it is man-centered. It centers on man himself. So, think about it—when you go on an internal pride search, you become self-focused. That often results in blindness concerning pride in your life. After all, if you're on this constant search to kill pride, you can't be proud, can you? If you hate pride and want to be rid of it, then you suddenly become proud of your humility, forgetting that all of your sin is pride.

Try to name one sin you can commit that doesn't have pride at the center of it—you can't. Since every sin is an act of defiance against God, you put pride to death by submitting yourself to God and by submitting yourself to His Word. We'll see in James 4 that the way to humility is the way of submission—submission to God in all of life, in all our ways, to all His Word.

In other words, true humility is not selective when it comes to sin. It is ready to put sin to death in all its forms. And as you go about dealing with sin in your life, you look away from yourself, you live a Christ-focused, God-focused, Scripture-obedient life, depending upon the Lord, as you look to God. He brings your sins before your mind's eye and you're able to confess them and deal with them. As you continue doing that, you'll be humbling yourself and your pride will be dealt with. And that's what the person meant who said, pride is a sin best slain indirectly.

We will see that this text demonstrates this. As we look at these verses, we'll note two problems, a divine solution, and then the fruits of applying the solution.

Reflection and Application

1. How can a person be boldly outspoken, like Peter, and at the same time be humble?
2. What is biblical hope? How is it different from wishful thinking or "possibility thinking"?
3. What's the difference between outward appearance (such as posture) and interior attitude?
4. Explain why you can never become humble by constantly searching yourself for pride that you can root out. Why is pride a sin that's best slain indirectly?

Two Problems

The Self-Driven Life

The first problem we see is that of **the self-driven life**. This is pride, the self-driven life.

James 4:1-3 *What causes quarrels and what causes fights among you? Is it not this, that your passions are at war within you? ² You desire and do not have, so you murder. You covet and cannot obtain, so you fight and quarrel. You do not have, because you do not ask. ³ You ask and do not receive, because you ask wrongly, to spend it on your passions.*

The word for *passions* here is a word for pleasures, the desire to please yourself. You can also substitute "selfishness," because I think that's the sense of what he's describing. It's a passion, a desire to please you.

The self-driven life is one of relational conflict. Whenever we live selfishly, we live in a way that brings conflict into our lives with other people. As James writes this, he's mindful, no doubt, of arguing, bickering, quarrels and dissensions among those to whom he writes. He's asking, "What causes this? What is the source of all this fighting? Is it not this: your desire to please you? Is it not your selfishness raging within you, at war within you? **The result of your selfishness is that you don't care about other people**. You desire and do not have, so you murder. I want what I want, and if you get in the way, you're expendable. I think he's using murder here in a figurative sense, in a metaphorical sense— "I will get rid of you if you get in the way of my desires. I'll trample upon you if you get in the way of my desires. I'm the most important person here, so, if you get in the way, I'll have to get you out of the way."

You not only don't care for others, but **you don't yield to others**, either. "You covet and cannot obtain," so what do you do? You "fight and quarrel." You don't give in, and don't yield. No one else is going to get their way. You're going to make sure you get your way, so you'll fight for your way.

When you don't care, you don't yield, and the result is, **you don't worship**, not with that attitude. There's no room, when you're in this mindset, for you to worship God. The self-driven life is a life of not asking God. *You do not have, because you do not ask* (vs. 2). What you desire in sin is not what God gives, so you don't seek Him for it. You intend to accomplish it on your own.

If you have a form of religion in these moments when you're living like this, and you ask God for something, *You ask and do not receive, because you ask wrongly* (vs. 3). What God gives, and what He is pleased to give, is that which is <u>good</u> for you, <u>good</u> for others, and <u>glorifying</u> to His name. But your selfishness is <u>not good</u> for you, <u>not good</u> for others, and it's <u>not glorifying</u> to His name. So even your prayers in these moments, these seasons of selfishness, will not be answered, <u>because you're asking wrongly.</u> You just want to fulfill your passions.

The World-Loving Life

The second way to describe the self-driven life is **the world-loving life**. You walk in step with lost humanity, with the standards of this world. This is the spirit at work in the sons of disobedience.

Eph. 2:1-2 *And you were dead in the trespasses and sins in which you once walked, following the course of this world, following the prince of the power of the air, the spirit that is now at work in the sons of disobedience.*

You adulterous people! says James in verse 4. Wait—what does he mean by *adulterous*? This is the kind of language you often find in the Old Testament prophets that speaks of a people being unfaithful to their God. They were in a covenant relationship with God, but now they're forsaking faithfulness to the covenant by pursuing the idolatry of the surrounding nations. Here in James 4, the people of God are pursuing life on the world's terms, the same way that a worldling would live, would think, and the same sorts of passions and desires he'd pursue.

This is unfaithfulness to God. For the believer, this is spiritual adultery. Putting it in the language of verse 4, when we choose a worldly life, we have chosen to stand in the position of God's enemies. *Do you not know that friendship with the world is enmity with God?* This kind of life is hateful to God. It's like declaring war Him. If you want to be *a friend to the world* and to live your life on the world's terms, with the world's ambitions and the world's ways, you make yourself *an enemy of God*. You can't worship God in this state. Whenever you're choosing to live like this, you're not living a life of worship. In fact, **you're trying to nullify God's desires to fulfill your own sinful desires.** God has a desire related to you, child of God. What is it? Read the next statement.

Or do you suppose it is to no purpose that the Scripture says, 'He yearns jealously over the spirit that he has made to dwell in us'? (vs. 5). What does that mean**? It means God's desire is for us. He wants us.** You belong to Him, and you've been purchased by Him, but in selfishness, you're giving yourself to the same course that characterizes a world that hates God and walks in opposition to Him. Are you teaming up with such a world? Don't you know that you're trying to nullify God's desires for you?

1 Co 6:19 *Or do you not know that your body is a temple of the Holy Spirit who is in you, whom you have from God, and that you are not your own?*

2 Co 6:16 *Or what agreement has the temple of God with idols? For we are the temple of the living God; just as God said, "I will dwell in them and walk among them; And I will be their God, and they shall be My people.*

Exodus 34:14 *(for you shall worship no other god, for the* LORD, *whose name is Jealous, is a jealous God)*

Reflection and Application

1. Why is a self-driven life never humble?
2. Why or how does a self-driven life lead to conflicts?

3. If you don't covet (that is, if you don't desire that you, instead of your neighbor, have something), how can you have enough?

4. Why might the humble person ask God for things—even material things—that the proud person wouldn't ask God for?

5. What's the difference between asking God rightly for something, and asking him wrongly for something?

6. People in past centuries often spoke of the dangers of worldliness. If you were trapped in worldliness, what do you think would be some signs? And what is the difference between worldliness and freedom in Christ?

7. For a Christian, in what way is loving the world spiritual adultery?

8. Some people think that when praying, they need to find the right formula to get God to do their will. They want to use God. Have you ever done that? Have you seen others doing that? Why is it a wrong-headed approach to prayer?

The Divine Solution

Pride is not some small thing. Do we wonder why God hates pride? It is idolatry, <u>as if you're on the throne instead of God being on His throne.</u> What is the solution for the believer who has found himself or herself fallen into the trap of a self-driven, world-loving life? And, by the way, if you don't know anything about this mindset, then you're not honest with your own condition. Have you ever been selfish? Have you ever been involved in arguments and fights and quarrels? If you're never involved in any of that, just say, "I'm wonderful!" But that wouldn't be a true statement.

We find the **divine solution** for this problem in verses 6-10: *But he gives more grace.* **Do you know what the answer is for our sin problem? It's grace.** He gives more grace, grace greater than our sin issues, grace more powerful if we will choose it, if we will yield to what God is willing to do for us. Grace that is sufficient for all our battles with sin. <u>He gives all the grace we could possibly need.</u>

What James has in mind here is not the grace of forgiveness, though obviously we need ongoing forgiveness, but <u>the grace of God's help.</u> This is grace that you could define as the power and the desire to do the will of God. What you need is God's grace to overcome YOURSELF. You need God's grace to overcome your own sinfulness and selfishness. You need God's grace to overcome your own idolatry, the idolatry of self. You need God's grace to live a different kind of life than the worldly life described in these verses.

Therefore it says, "God opposes the proud but gives grace to the humble" (vs. 6). And where do you find the grace of God? **The answer for the self-driven life, and the world-loving life, is the grace of God that is found in the place of humility.** The answer is grace, and you find access to that grace in the place of humility. *God opposes the proud, but He gives grace to the humble.* So then, what action do I take to experience humility? I need grace. I find it in the place of humility.

What steps would I take to walk in humility? Next statement: *Submit yourselves **therefore*** (vs. 7). Needing grace, you find it in humility. **Therefore**, here's what you do—you submit yourselves to God. Perhaps this idea is new to you, but try thinking about it like this. **If you want to know what humility is, it's submission to God.**

You'll never be humbler than when you honestly, from your heart, submit yourself to God by the standard of His Word. When you see God through His words for who He is, you'll see yourself in the light of truth, bow the knee, and submit yourself to Him by submitting to His words. You'll never see Him perfectly, but you'll see Him to the degree that you're able, given your maturity and progress in the Christian life. This is humility.

Where in God's Word are you fighting with God? What parts of God's Word do you politely listen to, and then ignore? What Words of God are you unwilling to be brought under the authority of, and power of? That's pride. Pride is wherever you set your will over God's will.

For example, think of Adam and Eve and the first temptation. What does Satan do? He questions and denies the words of God. What do Adam and Eve do? They give way to the voice of Satan, rejecting the words of God, and they fall.

By contrast, think of Christ's temptation by Satan in the wilderness. Satan quotes the words of God, but distorts them, questions them, and denies them. He offers Christ something in place of the promises of God. <u>But Jesus' response is to quote and to believe Scripture. He remains submitted to Scripture, and the devil has to flee.</u> The Son of God walks in perfect humility, fully submitted to the words of His Father. Adam and Eve fall through pride, refusing the wisdom of God. Where is your battle? Wherever you are disobeying Scripture, you are resisting God and cooperating with Satan. **Humility is found in the place of submission.**

Reflection and Application

1. If you think of God's jealous desire for us, is that a comfort to you? A challenge to you? Or both? Why?
2. What's the divine solution to our problem of sin and pride?
3. "You'll never be humbler than when you honestly, from your heart, submit yourself to God by the standard of His Word." Why is real humility linked to submission to God?

The Practical Results of Humility

Humility has practical results. The act of submission has many implications. From verse 7 to verse 10, there are ten commands. I believe the first command, the command to **Submit yourselves therefore to God** (vs. 7), is the domino that causes all the others to fall in this passage. If you obey the command to submit, you'll obey the commands that follow. Humility is found at the place of submission.

The next command is, **Resist the devil, and he will flee from you** (vs. 7). Again, we see that illustrated when we compare the temptation of Adam and Eve and the temptation of Christ. Adam and Eve do not submit themselves to God, and the devil celebrates over them. Jesus submits to the words of His Father, remains submitted, perfectly submitted, and the devil must flee. And so, as you submit yourself to God, you can experience victory over Satan. Humble yourself by submitting yourself to God and experience God's grace there. The result will be spiritual victory. This is how you have victory over Satan.

Further, you'll obey the command to **draw near to God** by submitting to Him. Not only will the devil flee, but you will be drawing near to your Father, and He will draw near to you. Has the sweetness disappeared from your walk with God? Has your nearness to God walked away? It left when your submission did, when you began to live selfishly instead of submissively. It left when you began to live in step with an unbelieving world instead of submitting your steps to the wisdom of God (James 3:13-18). Where are you not submitted to the words of God? Where in His Word right now are you aware of something you need to bow your knee to, something you need to obey, but you listen politely, acknowledge the truthfulness of Scripture, and choose to ignore it? Then you wonder why God seems so distant, imagining that somehow you can pick and choose which parts of God's Word you'll be submitted to, and yet have an overflowing sense of the nearness of God.

No, if you're really submitting yourself to God, there isn't one place in Scripture you aren't <u>willing</u>, and that's the key word, willing to be obedient to Him. "Lord, what is it that You would have me do? I will do it." That's submitting yourself to God. When you do that, when there is truly nothing off limits, nothing He couldn't call upon, nothing He couldn't identify. You say, "Show me, Lord, whatever it is where I'm out of step, and I will submit myself to You." <u>Now you're drawing near to God, and now He draws near to you.</u>

As we submit ourselves to the Lord, **we now know sensitivity to sin**. You *draw near to God and he will draw near to you*. What does this involve? It means you *cleanse your hands, you sinners, and purify your hearts*. That's done by submission to His Word. *You double-minded* (vs. 8)—Part of you wants to please God, and part of you wants to please yourself. As you see sin and confess sin, submitting to the words of God, and thus submitting yourself to your Father, do you realize what's happening? You are walking in the answer to the psalmist's prayer when he says, *Unite my heart to fear your name* (Ps 86:1).
"Wherever there is any duplicity in me, God, wherever

there's any division found in me, any inconsistency, would You unite me? Would You unite my heart to fear You and walk with You?"

This doesn't happen through some self-absorbed, morbid search within yourself, but by yielding to the Word of God wherever it calls for your submission. <u>The result is sorrow for sin.</u> *Be wretched and mourn and weep. Let your laughter be turned to mourning* (vs. 9). This is the world's sort of laughter, lighthearted living, without any concern as to whether you're pleasing God. It's living for yourself. Let that kind of laughter *be turned to mourning and your joy to gloom* (vs. 9).

One of the great lies about sin is that those who have lived in sin understand it better than those who are not living in it. Many years ago, I was part of a visitation team, and we entered the home of one dear lady. Behind her was a whole shelf full of witchcraft books. She told us that we could never understand Satan the way she could, because she's been involved with witchcraft. Satan is the enemy, yet she thought she understood the enemy as she was giving in to him. In other words, there was a blindness in her life.

Listen carefully—it's not those who are living in sin who best understand sin. Those people are inebriated by it, drunk on it. This is an amazing thing to realize: <u>The greater your submission to God, the greater your humility before God, the greater your sensitivity will be to that which displeases God.</u> And that sensitivity will not be chiefly a sensitivity to sin existing in others, but a sensitivity to sin existing in YOU. People who best understand sin are not people giving themselves to it, but those who are standing apart from it so that they aren't inebriated by it. It's only as we choose to confess and to turn from sin, *cleanse* our *hands*, *purify* our *hearts* by submission to the words of God, that sensitivity to sin now becomes prominent in our lives. <u>We have greater sensitivity to sin as we draw near to God.</u>

We need to examine submission in light of our sensitivity to sin. What has happened when our sensitivity to sin has walked away? What has happened when we are practicing things we once would have never practiced, are involved in things we once would have never been involved with, and are not made sorrowful by things that used to break our hearts? This behavior needs to be traced to the matter of submission. Have I humbled myself by truly submitting myself to God? Have I said, "God, whatever Your Word says, there I will bow my knee, and there my feet will travel."

Having victory over Satan, nearness to God, and sensitivity to sin, will result in **trusting God with your life**, with your status, and with whatever it is He wants to do with you. Verse 10: *Humble yourselves before the Lord, and he will exalt you.* What do you imagine it means when it says the Lord *will exalt you*? **He** will lift you up, take care of you, and sustain you. **He** will put you where He wants you to be and will make of your life what He wants it to be. That's exaltation. All we should want is what He wants. The best you'll ever have is God's will for your life. That's exaltation. <u>To be a faithful slave of Christ is exaltation.</u> One of the greatest reasons we fight with others is to establish a higher place for ourselves, unless we already have a higher place. Then, sometimes pride emerges, defending that place, trying to keep someone else down. So, can you trust the Lord? Instead of fighting and clawing for yourself, would you simply submit yourself to <u>all of His Word</u> in <u>all the realms of your life</u>, and then **trust Him for what He wants to do with you?** That's humility.

Reflection and Application

1. Do you believe there's a real devil? How can you distinguish between a fleshly temptation and a satanic temptation? (Or is that unnecessary?) How can you escape the devil's snares?
2. How does submission to God relate to nearness to God?
3. What does it mean to be double-minded? How can you have a united heart?
4. Have you ever spent time mourning over your sin? If not, consider setting aside a time to do that— honestly facing your sin, and then applying the Lord's promises of forgiveness, such as in 1 John 1:9.
5. Why does the person steeped in evil not really understand evil?
6. When you're interacting with other people, do you see a difference between those who are most sensitive to their own sin, and those who are most sensitive to other people's sin? How can we grow in seeing both ourselves and others as we really are?

7. Can you think of examples, whether in the Bible or elsewhere, where people have humbled themselves before the Lord, and then the Lord has exalted them?

The Fruits of True Humility

The solution to the self-driven life, and the world-loving life, is the humble life that is chosen by submission to God, and that life has some unmistakable, characteristic fruit. Beginning in verse 11 down to the end of the chapter, we see the **fruits of true humility**. *Do not speak evil against one another, brothers. The one who speaks against a brother or judges his brother, speaks evil against the law and judges the law* (vs. 11). If you're doing that, you've taken it upon yourself to do something the law would condemn. You've set yourself over the law, in the place of the law, and you do it in a way that sets your own judgment over the judgment of Scripture. You go beyond the Words of God. Instead of being submissive to God's Words, you stand in the place of God's Words. <u>In an appalling display of pride, you stand in the place of God.</u> How? The next verses show one of the ways.

But if you judge the law, you are not a doer of the law but a judge. There is only one lawgiver and judge, he who is able to save and to destroy. But who are you to judge your neighbor? (vs. 11-12). **One of the fruits of humility is that we stop biting and devouring each other.** We stop acting like we are God with respect to our neighbor. Here in James 4, we are told not to judge, but in I Cor. 5:12, there's an exhortation to judge those within the church. We don't judge outsiders, but those who are in the church, and the context of that statement is church discipline. That is, we are to honor God's Word by not allowing scandalous sin to go unchecked in the life of the congregation.

The context for this statement in James is different. It is about putting ourselves in the place of the Judge. The judging here in James is when we presume to know what we cannot know, and then presume to be able to assess what we cannot assess. It is pretending that we know the hearts of people, which we don't. Or, it is taking our own standards that are outside of Scripture and beyond what the words of God would say, and then imposing them on others as if that's the standard. "My standard is the standard. You live up to my standard, or you have disobeyed God." That is pride, and **the fruit of humility is to stop that behavior.** We ask ourselves the question, "Who am I to judge you like that?" Submission to God's words would make that sort of judging impossible. The type of attitude and spirit that submits to God's words, would find that impossible. When God makes you aware of your own sinfulness, you will take His words to be the final word. You won't compromise His Word, but you will understand the grace necessary for you and your fellow servants to obey that word. <u>You will be gracious, patient, and encouraging, even when you need to reprove someone.</u>

Another fruit of humility is that we will stop acting as if we're the ultimate orchestrators of our lives and of our daily or weekly plans. Pride is presumption toward people and even toward God's will. Notice verse 13 regarding presumption of God's will: *Come now, you who say, "Today or tomorrow we will go into such and such a town and spend a year there and trade and make a profit."* Do you know what you do not know? Do you know what you do not know regarding people, and what you do not know

34

regarding God's will? Is your life one of dependence on God, or yourself?

Verse 14: *yet you do not know what tomorrow will bring.* Can you tell me with all accuracy what tomorrow will bring, or, do you know that you don't know that? *What is your life?* Who are you? *You are a mist that appears for a little time and then vanishes.* Are you living your life without a sense of your own mortality? You're not big stuff. You're not even substantial at all. You're just a mist, and then you're gone.

So, here's what you ought to say: *Instead you ought to say, "If the Lord wills, we will live and do this or that"* (vs. 15). God calls us to make plans. We need to make decisions in this world. But in every decision we make, we need to know what we really are, and what we really aren't, so that we don't make our plans as if we're God. And in all our planning and decision making, pleasing the Lord needs to be preeminent. We need to seek His will regarding His decrees, and then beyond that, the will of His desires. *"If the Lord wills, we will live and do this or that."*

As it is, you boast in your arrogance (vs. 16). When people talk and plan and live as if they control the future, they are **boasting in arrogance**. And so, **this is the fruit of true humility: you are not presumptuous when it comes to your neighbor, nor when it comes to your own life.** You know what you don't know, looking to the One who knows everything, and you're ready to submit to Him at every point. That's humility. It doesn't live life as if God isn't sovereign.

So, we <u>don't</u> bite and devour, we <u>don't</u> live without a dependency on God, we <u>don't</u> live our lives without a sense of our mortality, and we <u>don't</u> presume.

The last thought about the fruit of humility is a positive one. <u>We listen to God and care what He wants.</u> Verse 16: *As it is, you boast in your arrogance*. Now, here's where we must listen carefully: *All such boasting is evil*. Do you believe that? Are you willing to see when this kind of boasting is happening in your life? And are you willing to listen when God says it's <u>evil</u>? When we bite and devour each other, are you willing to hear, "That's <u>evil</u>"? When you plan our life without a thought in the world of what God would want, what accords with His Word, or the fact that He holds tomorrow and we don't, do you understand that's <u>evil</u>? Listen to the word God uses. Take it into your heart. <u>It's evil.</u>

Finally, if you really know that, and believe it, you will want to do what's right. Verse 17: *So whoever knows the right thing to do and fails to do it, for him **it is sin.***

When you know that it's not right to bite and devour your neighbor, but do it, <u>it's sin.</u> When you know it's not right to plan your life as if you're God, but do it anyway, <u>it's sin.</u> When you refuse to bow your knee, resist the devil, draw near to God, confess your sins and trust God with your station in life, <u>it's sin.</u> When you're fighting and scratching in this self-driven life, living your life as if you're a worldling, in that moment, <u>it's sin.</u>

The height of pride is when you know what is right to do in the sight of God and you just say, "I don't want to," or, "I won't." *God opposes the proud but gives grace to the humble*. Where does humility start? The problems are clear. The divine solution is grace, and you find it in humility.

It all begins with that very first command: *Submit yourselves therefore to God*. You'll find that He draws near to you. You will find that you'll be more sensitive to sin, and you'll confess your sin. And you'll find that when you know what is right to do, by the grace of God, you'll desire to do it, and you'll choose to do it as God draws near to you.

Prayer

Father in heaven, thank You for these words that expose why we needed Christ to die on the cross for our sins. We think about what we saw, and then we look at these verses, and it becomes very clear to us why Jesus had to absorb Your wrath upon Himself on the tree in order for us to be acceptable before You, and to spend eternity with You. This life that is described in James 4 is who we are by nature from Adam. It's only Your saving grace that would totally change our orientation so that instead of a self-driven life we desire to please You, instead of a life lived according to the world's standards we submit to Scripture, instead of thinking that we control our destinies we desire to do Your will. And what we want more than anything is to be exalted in the sense that what You would most want for us is what we most want.

So, Lord, strengthen us to be that people, to recognize when the sin that we've read about is present, and to kill sin in all of its forms—and in that way, indirectly slay the giant of pride.

We ask for this in Jesus' name. Amen.

Reflection and Application

1. How does humility change how we talk about one another?
2. How does humility stop us from attacking ("biting and devouring") one another?
3. Has anyone ever corrected you in a gracious, patient and encouraging way? How did that impact your response to the correction?
4. How is godly planning different from the world's ways of planning? (Have you noticed that many of the best-known time management and planning experts are not sound Christians? How would their advice be different if they were mature believers?)
5. Can a Christian ever boast? (See also 1 Cor 1:31; 2 Cor 11:30)
6. Is there anything the Lord has been telling you to do, that you have neglected to do?
7. Are you willing to obey the Lord in everything today, and thus to become humbler?

THINKING OUR WAY HOME

How to Persevere
Through Suffering

A Study of Romans 8:22-25

Romans 8:18-25

[18] For I consider that the sufferings of this present time are not worth comparing with the glory that is to be revealed to us. [19] For the creation waits with eager longing for the revealing of the sons of God. [20] For the creation was subjected to futility, not willingly, but because of him who subjected it, in hope [21] that the creation itself will be set free from its bondage to corruption and obtain the freedom of the glory of the children of God. [22] For we know that the whole creation has been groaning together in the pains of childbirth until now. [23] And not only the creation, but we ourselves, who have the firstfruits of the Spirit, groan inwardly as we wait eagerly for adoption as sons, the redemption of our bodies. [24] For in this hope we were saved. Now hope that is seen is not hope. For who hopes for what he sees? [25] But if we hope for what we do not see, we wait for it with patience.

Destined to Suffer

Christians are destined to suffer. In verses 16 and 17 of Romans 8, the Spirit of God, through Paul, informs us that the children of God must suffer on their way to glory. There is no glorification with Christ apart from suffering with Christ.

The Spirit himself bears witness with our spirit that we are children of God, and if children, then heirs—heirs of God and fellow heirs with Christ, provided we suffer with him in order that we may also be glorified with him.

Suffering is necessary to our glorification, not because we are somehow earning it through suffering, but because suffering is the very nature of the Christian life. In salvation, God has taken us out of the world and brought us into union with His Son, thus guaranteeing our suffering on this side of glory. He has made us a new creation, and the result is that we are no longer in step with this lost and dying world of humanity, so the world no longer loves us. God has granted us His own desires, what He loves and hates, through the new nature and through the indwelling Holy Spirit.

Just as the world regarded Christ, so the world will regard us. Just as the world acted toward Christ, the world will act toward us. This is why those who have been saved can be identified by their suffering.

1 Thessalonians 3:1-4 says: *Therefore when we could bear it no longer, we were willing to be left behind at Athens alone, and we sent Timothy, our brother and God's*

coworker in the gospel of Christ, to establish and exhort you in your faith, that no one be moved by these afflictions. For you yourselves know that we are destined for this. For when we were with you, we kept telling you beforehand that we were to suffer affliction, just as it has come to pass, and just as you know.

This was basic training for early Christians. They would not only present the gospel and see people converted, they also followed up with exhortations to continue in the faith, with honest conversation saying that suffering would soon follow. Some will suffer more, some less. Some will suffer in more extreme ways, some in milder ways, but indeed all who desire to live godly in Christ Jesus will suffer persecution. We will suffer in ways that belong to the fallenness of this world. This suffering will include not just persecution, but all the heartaches, pains and difficulties that have happened as a result of the fall and the curses.

The question then is this: How does the child of God deal with that suffering? How has God ordained that we navigate the present trials and tribulations? God's plan for our perseverance is a thinking plan. We'll see this modeled by the Apostle Paul (the divinely-inspired human author of Romans) as he takes us into his own mind, his own pattern of reasoning. **In studying this passage, we can learn how to think our way home.**

In verse 18 he says, *For I consider*. In other words, "This is my thought process. These are my considerations. This is how I regard the present sufferings...." Using this phrase, he takes us into his own mind, into his own patterns of reasoning, and becomes the model for all of us. He says, *For I consider that the sufferings of this present time are not worth comparing with the glory that is to be revealed to us. For the creation waits with eager longing for the revealing of the sons of God. For the creation was subjected to futility, not willingly, but because of him who subjected it, in hope that the creation itself will be set free from its bondage to corruption and obtain the freedom of the glory of the children of God.*

In essence, Paul says, "When I think about my present sufferings, I think about future glory. I think about what belongs to the sons and daughters of God. I think about the inheritance that is ours. I think about the glorious nature of our future." This is not theoretical for Paul. At the very beginning of his ministry, he was told that he must suffer much for the sake of the Name—and suffer he did. He describes his sufferings in 2 Corinthians 11: 23-28:

… far more imprisonments, with countless beatings, and often near death. [24] Five times I received at the hands of the Jews the forty lashes less one. [25] Three times I was beaten with rods. Once I was stoned. Three times I was shipwrecked; a night and a day I was adrift at sea; [26] on frequent journeys, in danger from rivers, danger from robbers, danger from my own people, danger from Gentiles, danger in the city, danger in the wilderness, danger at sea, danger from false brothers; [27] in toil and hardship, through many a sleepless night, in hunger and thirst, often without food, in cold and exposure. [28] And, apart from other things, there is the daily pressure on me of my anxiety for all the churches.

Interestingly, next He personifies the creation and puts it, the material world that God has made—not people, not angels—on a witness stand, and the creation adds its testimony to his. He says the future will be so glorious that whatever we go through right now is not worthy to be compared to that. In fact, when we arrive there, today's troubles will not even be remembered—they will seem like nothing.

Then the creation says that it is standing on its tiptoes, as it were, looking forward to the day when the sons of God are revealed, because the day of our glorious freedom will be the day of its glorious freedom. Right now, it is subjected to the bondage of corruption, not because of anything it did, but because of Adam's sin, and God's choice to put it into that state of corruption. What we see on the planet, and in this universe, is the result of the choice of the One who subjected it to the bondage of corruption. To paraphrase, the creation is saying to us, "What awaits the children of God is glorious indeed, and we can't wait, because when you get your glory, we're going to get our glory." That means, not only will we be different, fit for eternity—body and soul, but God will provide for us a world in which to live which is also brand new.

This is not mythology, and not some sort of positive thinking exercise. These are not pie-in-the-sky platitudes meant to make us feel better. This is the truth. **The way to Christian courage and to Christian encouragement is not positive thinking. It is truthful thinking.** Paul is saying to us, in effect, "The way I navigate the present is with truth about the future." One day everything will be new. This is precisely what we are told from the very throne of God.

Consider Revelation 21:3-5: *And I heard a loud voice from the throne saying, "Behold, the dwelling place of God is with man. He will dwell with them, and they will be his people, and God himself will be with them as their God. He will wipe away every tear from their eyes, and death shall be no more, neither shall there be mourning, nor crying, nor pain anymore, for the former things have passed away." And he who was seated on the throne said, "Behold, I am making all things new." Also he said, "Write this down, for these words are trustworthy and true."*

So, the most glorious aspect of our future is that we will see our Savior face to face, having unhindered fellowship with God. In some ways our future cannot be explained to us because we are insufficient to grasp it. Rather, God must define it for us in terms of what it will not be—no more death, no more mourning, no more crying, and no more pain. *For the former things have passed away. And he who was seated on the throne said, "Behold, I am making all things new.* That's what our future will be—everything new." Again, this is not positive thinking, but truthful thinking. This is also how Paul navigates his sufferings, and how we are meant to navigate ours: by preaching the truth to our own hearts, by preaching the truth about our future right in the face of our present difficulties.

But that thinking process requires something. In verses 22-25 of Romans 8, we find two bedrock elements upon which this thinking process relies—knowledge and faith. We are on our way to our final destination, but we are not there yet, and on the way, we are passing through many trials, tribulations and struggles, including persecution. How do we think our way home? <u>We think our way home on the foundation of knowledge and faith.</u>

Notice verses 22-23: *For we know that the whole creation has been groaning together in the pains of childbirth until now. And not only the creation, but we ourselves, who have the firstfruits of the Spirit, groan inwardly as we wait eagerly for adoption as sons, the redemption of our bodies.* <u>He says, *For we **know***, and then he says in verse 24, *For in this **hope** we were saved.*</u>

This knowledge is a kind that represents hope, which is to say it is a kind of knowledge that requires faith. Paul describes the nature of hope in the next statements: *Now hope that is seen is not hope. For who hopes for what he sees? But if we hope for what we do not see, we wait for it with patience.*

This is the process, the pathway, by which we navigate our present sufferings: We **think** about them rightly because we **know** what God has revealed, and we **believe** what God has revealed. We think a certain way because of what we know, but just knowing it is not enough. We think about it in light of what we know, because we believe what God has revealed. The fruit of this will then be shown in our attitudes, our words, and our actions.[1]

---

[1] This process of right thinking that comes from knowing and believing, leading to right doing, is true of all Christian sanctification.

Reflection and Application

1. "Christians are destined to suffer." Have you seen this in your own life? Were you warned of this when you became a believer?
2. What are some of the ways that you or those around you have tried to deal with the fact of experiencing suffering?
3. What are two things that made the apostle Paul an authority on the matter of suffering? (Hint: Consider the words <u>authority</u> and <u>suffering</u> as they relate to him.)
4. When you look at the world around you, do you see beauty or brokenness or both?
5. How does Adam's sin (Genesis 3) relate to this broken world?
6. Why will the creation be glad when God's children are revealed?
7. Is there a difference between positive thinking and truthful thinking? If so, what is it? How do you know the difference?
8. What will be the most glorious part of our future, if we're really trusting Jesus Christ?

The Believer's Knowledge (8:22-23)

The believer's knowledge is the first element in thinking our way home. Look again at verses 22-23: *For we know that the whole creation has been groaning together in the pains of childbirth until now. And not only the creation, but we ourselves, who have the firstfruits of the Spirit, groan inwardly as we wait eagerly for adoption as sons, the redemption of our bodies*.

Paul had spoken in verse 18 of his own thought process: *For I consider….* Notice that Paul now moves on from how he thinks, to the basis for it, and makes this a matter of Christian doctrine. He expands beyond just what he himself thinks, to what we know. He thinks as he does because *we know* something (vs. 22). He doesn't think this way because of some private knowledge or personal intuition, but because of a knowledge that has been made available to all of the children of God, something we all know.

This knowledge can be broken down into two categories: **what we know about the creation** and **what we know about ourselves.**

What we know about the creation (vs. 22)

He begins with the creation: *For we know that the whole creation has been groaning together in the pains of childbirth until now*. That is, it is **still** true as he writes this letter, and it is **still** true today as I write this small book. This is something we **still** know: the creation is groaning.

When he says that the creation is groaning, on the one hand, it speaks of the present frustration of creation—desires not satisfied. What is, is not what we could wish it would be, nor what it will one day be. Right now, there is a frustration that belongs to the way things are. That's one kind of groaning.

But in this groaning there is also another viewpoint, one that looks forward. We could describe it as longing, and that's why it's described in the terms of the pains of childbirth. *For we know that the whole creation has been groaning together in pains of childbirth....* When a woman is in labor, there is pain and suffering, but there's also anticipation, expectation, and a joyful looking forward, because as soon as the baby is born, there is joy. So, this groaning represents desire now frustrated, but still looking forward to the day when it will be fulfilled. It is longing for the day that God has promised to His children. On that day, creation will join us and know its liberation along with ours.

Everett Harrison and Donald Hagner, commenting on this, wrote: "The groaning of the creation looks back to its subjection to frustration (v. 20), whereas 'the pains of childbirth' anticipate the age of renewal. In other words, the same sufferings are at once a result and a prophecy. Jesus spoke of the renewing of the world and called it a 'regeneration'"[2]

---

[2] Everett F. Harrison and Donald A. Hagner, "Romans," in *The Expositor's Bible Commentary: Romans–Galatians (Revised Edition)*, ed. Tremper

The creation groans. Notice the details of this groaning. **First of all, what he describes can be seen in all creation.** Verse 22 says, *For we know that the whole creation has been groaning….* That is, there is not one part of the material universe that has not been affected by sin. Right now, there is not one aspect of it that expresses the fullness of what God has planned for it. There is a better day coming when the created order will fully reflect God's everlasting plan for what He has made, but that time is not now. Right now, we see a created order that is in the bondage of corruption.

Second, Paul describes a uniform groaning. He says, *For we know that the whole creation has been groaning **together** in the pains of childbirth….* I think the next verse makes it clear that the word *together* refers to us—redeemed humanity. Not only the creation groans, but we ourselves groan inwardly. So, the personified creation is pictured groaning along with the redeemed sons and daughters of God, because our future day will be its future day. And yet, because the whole creation groans together with us, we can still say there is uniformity in the created order itself. It is like a great choir singing this mournful, but hopeful message as it longs for and waits for the revealing of the sons of God.

Can we see any manifestation of that groaning, of this longing in creation for what God has promised? I think we

---

Longman III & Garland, David E., vol. 11 (Grand Rapids, MI: Zondervan, 2008), 138.

can. Our Lord talked about birth pains in what is known as the Olivet discourse. Matthew 24:3-14 says this:

As he sat on the Mount of Olives, the disciples came to him privately, saying, "Tell us, when will these things be, and what will be the sign of your coming and of the end of the age?" And Jesus answered them, "See that no one leads you astray. For many will come in my name, saying, 'I am the Christ,' and they will lead many astray. And you will hear of wars and rumors of wars. See that you are not alarmed, for this must take place, but the end is not yet. For nation will rise against nation, and kingdom against kingdom, and there will be famines and earthquakes in various places. All these are but the beginning of the birth pains. Then they will deliver you up to tribulation and put you to death, and you will be hated by all nations for my name's sake. And then many will fall away and betray one another and hate one another. And many false prophets will arise and lead many astray. And because lawlessness will be increased, the love of many will grow cold. But the one who endures to the end will be saved. And this gospel of the kingdom will be proclaimed throughout the whole world as a testimony to all nations, and then the end will come."

In these verses Christ is giving a panoramic view of the ages that lead up to the end of the age. <u>One of the ways that creation *groans* is the presence of difficulties and disasters that will not belong to the perfect world that is coming.</u> This will include times of trouble, heartache, pain, loss, spiritual deception, disloyalty, and mistreatment of others. There will be natural disasters such as earthquakes, hurricanes, and tornadoes, as well as famines and diseases. In other words, as this world reflects its fallenness, as it reflects the curse, the groaning is on display. Everything we can see in this world that is not as it will be, is a reminder that this is not the end—there's a better day coming. That's the groaning.

Have you noticed how this world of lost humanity wants to explain this groaning? When they look at what is happening on the planet, some think, "The planet is self-destructing, and things are getting hotter—or colder—due to climate change, and everything is falling apart." Their explanation for all this is us—man. They think it's not our sin against God, but our sins against creation. Their mindset is that there is nothing wrong with creation. Creation does not reflect a bondage to which God has subjected it. No, they think, "Creation is pristine. It's perfect. If we could just get man out of the way! There's no God in control of all this! No, man must deliver the creation himself, and the way we preserve the planet is by getting ourselves out of the way."

But that is a sinful and deceived mindset. God tells us that the problems we'll witness on this planet until the day Jesus comes, speak of a bondage to corruption that came about as a result of God's choice, not man's. Adam's sin led to this, but it was God Himself who chose to curse creation, and it groans under that curse until the day when God chooses to remove it. We won't remove it. We don't preserve the planet, and we won't fix the planet. God is the one who created it. He is the One who sustains it and is the One who one day will completely renovate it. We look to Him.

So, this is a uniform groaning that takes all of creation into account. This groaning not only reflects the present corruption, but **also anticipates a better day.**

Childbirth, what an illustration this is! It's as if the entire universe is writhing in pain, waiting for the day when the baby of God's perfect plans is delivered. The very One who subjected it, subjected it in hope (vs. 20), and that hope looks forward to God's plan for His redeemed sons and daughters (vs. 21) and for the world in which they will live. And when that day arrives, it is a birthday!

The very One who subjected it, subjected it in hope. That is, from the time when the curses were first pronounced, God's salvation plan was already being worked out, and there is this anticipation, this longing, for a new day that is described in verse 19: *For the creation waits with eager longing for the revealing of the sons of God*. A new day is coming.

Martyn Lloyd-Jones, commenting on this, said:

> I wonder whether the phenomenon of the Spring supplies us with a part answer. Nature every year, as it were, makes an effort to renew itself, to produce something permanent; it has come out of the death and the darkness of all that is so true of the Winter. In the Spring it seems to be trying to produce a perfect creation, to be going through some kind of birth-pangs year by year. But unfortunately, it does not succeed, for Spring leads only to Summer, whereas Summer leads to Autumn, and Autumn to Winter. Poor old nature tries every year to

defeat the "vanity," the principle of death and decay and disintegration that is in it. But it cannot do so. It fails every time. It still goes on trying, as if it feels things should be different and better; but it never succeeds. So it goes on "groaning and travailing in pain together until now." It has been doing so for a very long time . . . but nature still repeats the effort annually.[3]

What a great quote! This is a vivid picture of the kind of groaning that Paul is describing here, how the creation groans now in its subjection to the bondage of corruption.

<u>So, the knowledge of what is in store for this world strengthens us to think rightly about this present age.</u> And, by the way, if you think this knowledge isn't practical in nature, just take note of the world in which you're living. There is the issue of global warming and a world of people full of anxieties concerning the future of the planet. Yet, at the same time, a world of people full of false hopes. They think that somehow we'll rescue the planet, somehow we'll change the climate, and somehow we'll produce a world free from all of the manifestations of sin that we see among people.

God tells us that not only is the planet troubled, along with the human beings who live on it, but He tells us how it all came to pass. He tells us how He made it all, when the

---

[3]John MacArthur, *Romans 1–8*, The MacArthur New Testament Commentary; Accordance electronic ed. (Chicago: Moody Press, 1991), 457-458.

fall occurred, and what the result was in terms of the curses. God tells us what it will be like until the day when Jesus returns. He tells us that Christ will usher in a future new world, and He tells us what that new world will be like. So, we can live our lives in peace and confidence, in the rest that knows what is happening.

But without God's Word, people don't know what is happening. They don't know how it all came to be nor where it's all headed. And so, they're just left with what they're seeing right now in our world.

So, to think the right thoughts, we have to know what God has told us about creation. But there's more.

Reflection and Application

1. Why is knowledge important in the Christian life?
2. What do we know about creation?
3. In what ways have you seen the creation "groan-ing" in the past few days?
4. What parts of creation groan?
5. How is it that we, as God's redeemed children, groan along with creation? That is, how can we say that we groan together?
6. Is Mother Nature angry with us? Why or why not?
7. Why would the planet stay broken, even if there were no people left? (What will it take to fix the planet? Who can do that?)
8. How are typical "natural" disasters similar to birth-pains?
9. What does the creation anticipate? (Have you been accustomed to thinking of it in this way?)

What we know about ourselves (vv. 23-24a)

We also need to know what God has told us about ourselves. Not only do we know that a personified creation longs for its liberation, we know a longing within our own hearts.

Verse 23: *And not only the creation, but **we ourselves**, who have the firstfruits of the Spirit, groan inwardly as we wait eagerly for adoption as sons, the redemption of our bodies.*

Paul says, *we wait eagerly for adoption as sons*, yet he told us earlier that we are already adopted ones. How do we put these two things together? If you know Jesus Christ as Lord and Savior, you are already adopted—you already belong to the family of God. But the full manifestation of our status as those adopted sons and daughters has not yet come about. One day in this world it will be fully revealed who are the children of God, and in that sense our adoption will have been brought to completion. And that future adoption is put to us in terms of resurrection, that we're looking forward to the redemption of our bodies. But right now, we groan. We groan over the sins of this world. We groan over the sins of our own life. We groan over our weak condition due to the effects of the fall, and our exposure to all of the dangers that belong to this fallen world. We grieve over the sickness, the pain, and the death that we must experience in this world.

We find ourselves longing for something permanent, as Martyn Lloyd-Jones put it; longing for a new day that will never end. This longing is fueled by the taste of that new day. God has given us His Spirit, and we have the firstfruits of the Spirit—we already have everlasting life. We each received eternal life the day we were saved, but what we do not yet have is everything that has been promised in association with that everlasting life. That day is coming. We long for it now, and the very presence of the Spirit of God enables us to see that future with the eyes of faith and to long for it with a transformed heart.

We have also had a taste of that new life in another sense. Because He lives in us, He is also producing in us the kind of character that will one day be fully manifest in our lives. Right now, we are being conformed to the image of Christ, and one day we'll see Him face to face. And when we see Him, we will be like Him. John MacArthur put it well when he said this: Just as the first pieces of produce to appear on a tree provide hope of a future harvest, the fruit which the Spirit produces in us now (Gal 5:22, 23) provides hope that we will one day be like Christ.[4]

When we see the Holy Spirit producing in us love, joy, peace, patience, gentleness, kindness, and self-control, all those things listed in Galatians 5, this is the first taste of what we know He will be faithful to produce in us as He conforms us to the image of His Son. It's not only the creation groaning, having a type of frustration in the present, with a hope for the future. You and I also know a kind of frustration in the present, but with a hope for the future,

---

[4] John F. MacArthur Jr., *The MacArthur Study Bible: New American Standard Bible.* (Nashville, TN: Thomas Nelson Publishers, 2006), Ro 8:23.

because we have the Spirit of God living in us. We long for that day and look forward to it eagerly. As Paul says, *we wait eagerly...for the redemption of our bodies* (vs. 23).

One day, we will have a new physical existence that will match what God has done in our souls. God's plan for humanity from the very beginning was for a creature that is both spiritual and physical in nature—body and soul. Right now, we know a transformation in our souls, but we each have a body that still experiences the flesh, the sin principle. We know the aging, the sicknesses, and the death that belong to this mortal body, but one day we will each have a transformed body that matches the new us, and we long for that day to arrive.

We think with this knowledge in mind—what we know about the creation and about ourselves— and then we preach those truths to ourselves even in the midst of present heartache.

Reflection and Application

1. Explain "firstfruits."
2. What does the Holy Spirit mean in your life?
3. Would those closest to you say that you are growing in the fruit of the Spirit (see Galatians 5:22-23)?
4. How does the fruit of the Spirit point to a future of being like Christ?
5. Do you often preach to yourself? If so, what are you preaching to yourself?
6. Maybe you are preaching to yourself what people and your feelings say is true, or maybe you are preaching to yourself what the Bible says is true. What difference will there be in the results?

The Believer's Hope (8:24-25)

Paul has been talking about knowledge, and in verse 24 he talks about the nature of that knowledge. What kind of knowledge is this? We know things about creation and about ourselves. We know we can look forward to a new world and a new body. How do we know this?

He reveals it in verse 24 when he says that it was *in this hope we were saved*. He then goes on to explain what hope is. *Now hope that is seen is not hope*. Hope is about a different kind of sight, not what we see with our eyes, but what we see based purely and entirely on God's words.

If all we had was the knowledge we could gain by our senses, we could know that something is very wrong in this world, but we could never explain what it is, how all these problems came to be. And we could never understand the solution for it. We would have no access to God's plan for all that exists. For instance,

- How do we know how the world came into existence? We weren't there.
- How do we know how the world came to be in its current state of corruption? We weren't there to see how it happened.
- Why is the world in its present condition?
- How do we know our view of it is true?
- Where is the created order headed?
- What is going to be its future?
- Is there going to be a new world one day? How do we know?

- How do we know these things about creation?

And, by the way, how do we know that one day we're going to experience a resurrection? How do we know salvation is real, that our sins are really forgiven, that we've really been united with Christ, that we really have the Spirit of God, and we're going to have a new body that matches that reality? How do we know all this?

God told us. His revelation to us is the only way we know it—His words. **When we live our lives resting entirely on God's Word, that is hope. And that hope will not be disappointed, because we have put our faith in the words of a God Who cannot lie and Who is altogether good, so that what we have staked our lives on is truth.**

This is how we are meant to live the Christian life — by God's design. We don't live the Christian life by sight, but by hope. We live the Christian life by faith. If all we were left with is what we could see, we would never be able to explain this world. If we could only know what we can see, we would never be able to envision our future. But God has told us what it will be, and therefore, we have this knowledge. **The nature of the knowledge is that it rests entirely on the words of God, so that it becomes a knowledge that we have by faith.**

Hope belongs to salvation

Notice that Paul says hope belongs to salvation. He says in verse 24: *For in this hope we were saved.* It was not until the Lord saved us that we had hope or had the capacity to live in hope. The Christian life, by God's design, is meant to be a life of hope. We are not waiting on these things because we have chosen for it to be so, but because God has chosen for it to be so. Hope is a part of Christian living because God designed it so.

These promises belong to us only because we're in Jesus Christ. If you're not in Christ today, then these promises are not yours. What you can expect is not a glorious new world full of all kinds of beauty and variety in which God will be your God forever.

No, without Christ you can expect that you'll be in hell, a place of everlasting separation from God, everlasting torment. If you're not in Christ, you can expect a resurrection, but you're not going to be raised to live forever in heaven. You'll be raised to be cast body and soul into hell. If you don't know Jesus Christ, you'll be given a physical existence fit for eternal suffering.

Hope requires faith

The only way this hope becomes your hope is through faith in the Lord Jesus Christ. He's the only Savior given to men, the eternal Son of God who left heaven, came to earth, took to Himself an additional nature, a perfect human nature. He lived a sinless life under the law, died in the stead of sinners on the cross, has been raised from the dead bodily, and saves forever sinners who will look to Him by faith. By putting your faith in Him, this becomes your hope.

It was in this hope, then, that we were saved. We were introduced into it when we were saved, and then Paul says it does indeed require faith. *Now hope that is seen is not hope. For who hopes for what he sees? But if we hope for what we do not see, we wait for it with patience.*

The life we are living is not a life explained by sight. Here is something that may help you when you think about preaching these truths to yourself regarding the future. <u>Understand this: the same principle by which you love the Lord Jesus Christ today is the principle by which you can long for your future.</u>

If you love Jesus, how did you come to love Him? It was God Who granted you the new birth, and with it came the eyes of faith. You have never seen Jesus or touched Him. The only way you know Jesus is with the eyes of faith, and it is by those eyes that you love Him. In the same way, you have never seen the future that is coming. You have never yet seen nor experienced those things God has promised. You have no way to even relate to them on that level, but God has told you, and now with the eyes of faith that He has granted you, you are able to take hold of those things and live in the expectation of them.

That's exactly what the Apostle Peter told us in 1 Peter 1:3-9 when he wrote this: *Blessed be the God and Father of our Lord Jesus Christ! According to his great mercy, he has caused us to be born again to a living hope through the resurrection of Jesus Christ from the dead, to an inheritance that is imperishable, undefiled, and unfading, kept in heaven for you, who by God's power are being guarded through faith for a salvation ready to be revealed in the last time. In this you rejoice, though now for a little while, if necessary, you have been grieved by various trials so that the tested genuineness of your faith—more precious than gold that perishes though it is tested by fire—may be found to result in praise and glory and honor at the revelation of Jesus Christ. Though you have not seen him, you love him. Though you do not now see him, you believe in him and rejoice with joy that is inexpressible and filled with glory, obtaining the outcome of your faith, the salvation of your souls.*

If you are capable of loving the Son of God, then you are capable of longing for the future that God has given you in His Son. <u>That is how we are called to live, not by putting our eyes on our present troubles, sorrows, hardships, loss and grief, but by putting our eyes on the future that God has promised.</u> We **think** that way because we know what God has told us about creation and about ourselves. And now we **believe** Him, and by believing Him, we are living that life of hope. Knowledge is not enough. <u>We can know what is true, but if we don't believe it, if we don't grasp hold of it with our hearts, then it will never transform the way we live.</u>

Hope rests in God's Word

Besides belonging to salvation and requiring faith, <u>hope rests in the Word of God.</u> Notice how Paul describes our waiting in verse 25: *But if we hope for what we do not see, we wait for it with patience*. That is to say, this life of faith is a life of endurance. We don't believe just once or for just a little while. We continue waiting for what God has promised with perseverance, with patience, trusting that God will bring it about at the perfect time. We are not waiting because we want to wait, but because it's what God has chosen for us. He has chosen that we live this life of hope.

The only way to do this is by not only believing His words, but by resting in them.

We don't wait for the future by putting it out of our minds—"You know, it's really hard right now, and I know there's a better day coming, but it almost pains me to think about the better day, so I'm going to put the better day out of my mind and just concentrate on navigating today's troubles." That's not the Christian life. Instead, it is, "I'm going to navigate today's troubles with my future squarely in my sights. I'm going to fix my mind on the Lord Jesus Christ and the hope of what He's going to produce in our lives when He arrives."

Paul describes this in 2 Corinthians 4:18 and following. He says, *as we look not to the things that are seen but to the things that are unseen. For the things that are seen are transient, but the things that are unseen are eternal.*

How do we look at what we can't see? By faith, by fixing our eyes on that which will be forever, and that includes our bodies, too. Continuing in 2 Corinthians to chapter 5 verses 1-9, *For we know that if the tent that is our earthly home is destroyed, we have a building from God, a house not made with hands, eternal in the heavens.* In this passage, God through Paul, tells us about our bodies—their nature in the present, here on earth, and what they'll be like in heaven.

The tent he is describing is the tent of your body. Right now, we are living a mortal existence, but there is an eternal existence that God has already prepared for us. Verse 2, *For in this tent we groan, longing to put on our heavenly dwelling, if indeed by putting it on we may not be found naked. For while we are still in this tent, we groan, being burdened—not that we would be unclothed, but that we would be further clothed….*

Paul means what we are longing for is not just some spiritual existence—floating around without a body. As I said, God made us to exist body and soul, and we long for a new body fit for eternity that will match our spiritual condition. What we long for, he says here in verse 4, is *that what is mortal may be swallowed up by life*. That is, our longing is for a body that never dies, that which is permanent. And, continuing in the verses…

[5] *He who has prepared us for this very thing is God, who has given us the Spirit as a guarantee.* [That is, the firstfruits, the first taste of what will be our forever future.]

[6] *So we are always of good courage. We **know*** [there's that beautiful word again that we saw in verse 22 of our text. Here's what we know:] *We **know** that while we are at home in the body we are away from the Lord,* [7] *for we walk by faith, not by sight*. [That's our present way to live.] [8] *Yes, we are of good courage, and we would rather be away from the body and at home with the Lord*.

We long for the day when this stage of God's plan for creation is done. We long for the day, just as the creation does, when we will see the liberation, both of the sons of God and of the created order, at the same time. There will be a new world in which the redeemed ones will live, but until then, there is one thing that always stays the same.

Finally, look at 2 Corinthians 4:9. *So whether we are at home or away, we make it our aim to please him*. How do we live until we get there? We live in a way that says, "Lord, I want to please You in all my ways—in my thinking, my attitudes, my choices, and my behaviors. I want to please You. And one day when I stand before You face to face, my aim will not change. There I will want to hear, 'Well done. Well done.'"

This is how you and I think our way home, how we are meant to navigate our way through the present sufferings. We think about the greatness of the glory of our future and consider that our joy in the future will make today's sorrows something to forget. **We think right thoughts based on the truth, on what we know—**because we have the right information, and **because we believe it.** We believe what God has revealed about the world in which we're living. We don't live thinking that what is happening is because of our sins against creation, or somehow we're going to usher in this glorious new planet because we didn't drive cars, or because we put up solar panels to power our houses, or because we've put up a bunch of windmills to produce energy. No, we're not trying to usher in a new planet. **We know** who made it, and we know what went wrong with it. **We know** how it exists to this very day. We hang onto the very words of Jesus, upheld by His very Word, and **we know** where it's all headed.

Nor do we imagine that there's any way to transform society without salvation. Our hope is not in politicians and not in social movements. **We have one confidence—what God says is true.** The world was made the way He said, and it went wrong the way He said. It exists the way He says, and it's headed toward what He says. **The only answer for this world of humanity is Jesus, salvation in Christ.** That produces a new humanity—a redeemed humanity—and a new unity that's not found in something as superficial as skin color. There is one kind of human being descended from Adam and Eve, one kind of saved human being— someone united to Jesus Christ and indwelt by the Spirit of God.

We don't get this information from the world. We get it from God's Word. The question to each of us is, do you believe it? **We think the right thoughts because we know the right information, and we believe what God has revealed. That's how we think our way home.**

Reflection and Application

1. What is biblical hope? How is it different from wishful thinking or "possibility thinking"?
2. What does Christian hope rest on?
3. "Hope belongs to salvation." Why is the Christian's hope available only to those who are saved? (Are you sure you're saved, rescued from sin? If not, read Romans 10:9-10 and Acts 16:30-31.)
4. Consider and explain the statement, "The same principle by which we love the Lord Jesus Christ today is the principle by which we can long for our future."
5. How often do you long for the future that God has promised? If the answer is, "Seldom," how can faith in God transform your thinking?
6. What does it mean to rest in God's Word?
7. What do we know about our bodies in the resurrection? And how can that help us now?